TheFieldMouse
Collection

The Field Mouse Collection

The Field
Mouse

Clem Martini

Playwrights Canada Press
Toronto • Canada

Playwrights Canada Press

54 Wolseley St., 2nd floor Toronto, Ontario CANADA M5T 1A5
416-703-0013   fax 416-703-0059
orders@playwrightscanada.com • www.playwrightscanada.com

Playwrights Canada Press acknowledges the support of
the taxpayers of Canada and the province of Ontario through
The Canada Council for the Arts and the Ontario Arts Council.

Cover photos by Trudie Lee. *The Field* (l to r) Sanjay Talwar, Kevin
Rothery, Nikki Lundmark, Susan McNair Reid. *Mouse* (l to r) Matthew
Kennedy, Cam Ascroft, Shannon Anderson, Kathy Fraser.
Production Editor/Cover Design: Jodi Armstrong

National Library of Canada Cataloguing in Publication Data

Martini, Clem, 1956-
    The field mouse collection : two plays : The field & mouse / Clem
Martini.

ISBN 0-88754-648-X

    1. Children's plays, Canadian (English) I. Title.

PS8576.A7938F53 2002   jC812'.54   C2002-902589-3
PZ7

First edition: September 2002.
Printed and bound by AGMV Marquis at Quebec, Canada.

ACKNOWLEDGEMENTS

This collection is the result of many people's efforts. I should thank Artistic Director Duval Lang whose excellent theatre for young people, Quest Theatre, produced the premiere of both pieces. I should thank Angela Rebeiro, Publisher of Playwrights Canada Press, for her efforts to make this collection happen. I would like to thank JoAnne James for her very gracious words. The Alberta Foundation for the Arts should be thanked for their assistance along the way, and as always I thank my wife, Cheryl Foggo, and my children Chandra and Miranda for their comments, their attentiveness, and their superhuman patience.

INTRODUCTION

Clem Martini loves kids. He treats his audiences the way he treats his own daughters, with the utmost respect for their intelligence. The plays he writes for children are challenging, funny and provocative.

Mouse raises questions about conformity and peer pressure within the unique confines of a cage of mice. *The Field* examines the birth of a new friendship taking place in the shadow of racism. Both plays present the kind of strong independent characters that kids want to emulate. Both plays make kids think.

Clem has been a valued friend and a colleague of mine for more than twenty years. He is one of the brightest, most compassionate people I know. I have had the privilege of watching him become a fine writer and an extraordinary parent.

We have often talked about the odd pressure that exists to label him as either a "kids writer" or a "serious writer," but the simple truth is that he writes for people, young and old. Clem has the capacity to write with a child's voice, but I am convinced that both *The Field* and *Mouse* resonate for all ages. Pigeonholes? They're for pigeons.

JoAnne James
Artistic Director / Producer
The Calgary International Children's Festival

TABLE OF CONTENTS

The Field

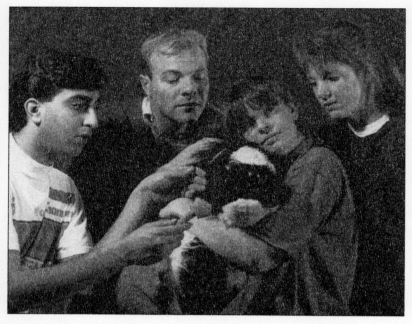

(l to r) Sanjay Talwar, Kevin Rothery, Nikki Lundmark, Susan McNair Reid. Photo by Trudie Lee.

The Field was first produced by Quest Theatre, touring Alberta, 1991-92 season, with the following cast and crew:

ARUN   Sanjay Talwar
BEN   Kevin Rothery
LANE   Nikki Lundmark
BLAZE   Susan McNair Reid

Directed by Duval Lang
Set, Costumes and Lighting designed by Jim Wills
Sound designed by Michael Becker
Stage Managed by Susan McNair Reid

CHARACTERS

LANE MARSHALL
A nine-year-old girl. Blind, but extremely self sufficient.

BEN MARSHALL
Lane's older brother by two years.

ARUN SOOD
A boy the same age as Lane. Arun's parents come from India.

BLAZE
Lane's dog. A life sized, hand operated puppet.

SETTING

A field on the outskirts of the city, located on land slated to be developed. Because trees surround it, one is left with the impression that this piece of land is situated further out in the country than it really is. Once, long ago, it had a house on it, but the house has since been abandoned and fallen into disrepair.

SCENE ONE

> *LANE stands listening. BLAZE, her dog, lies sleeping a few feet from her. In her hands LANE holds a sprig of a spruce tree, some cedar and some pine. She sniffs them, and passes them to the audience to examine as well.*

LANE   Smell.

That's what the field smelled like. It smelled of spruce, and of pine, and cedar so strong that it was almost like a blanket over top of everything else.

This is the story of what happened in the field. It was only a few blocks from our new house, the house that we'd just moved into that summer, but it felt like it was miles and miles away. Like it was way out in the country.

This–

> *She gestures around her.*

–is the field. It's big. I can run from one side to another in seventy five steps, this way. And a hundred and twenty steps that way. Trees all along the edges, that's where the smells come from. And then mostly tall grass, covering the field, like this–

> *She holds some up.*

–kind of, rattling—is that the right word?—when the wind blows. Tickling your face and neck and arms when you crawl through it.

> *She allows some of the audience to feel the grass. She steps back and strokes BLAZE.*

This is Blaze, my dog.

> *BLAZE looks up and around, pants, and flops back down.*

The field is full of things. Plants and ants and berries and things like that, but also people's things. Old things. Ben, my brother, found a glass bottle from maybe fifty, sixty years ago that a neighbour said might be worth some money or maybe a museum would be interested in even. I found this.

She pulls a spoon from her pocket and feels it carefully.

It's old too, and silver, and has these curly cues at the end of it. There's a shack at the far end of the field, over there. I call it a shack. It must have been some-one's house once, just like this must have been some-one's yard. Garden. Whatever. When it rains I can still come to the field if I want and keep dry because of the shack. When the sun beats down like today, I can do any old thing I want. Carve things with this pocket knife, gather up rocks like these–

She spills a bag of rocks onto the ground.

I like the smooth ones – braid a cedar whip, or just lie around and think about things.

> *LANE sits and leans against BLAZE. She takes a cucumber out of her jacket pocket, cuts off a few slices, eats some, then places two slices over her eyes. She leans back contentedly. ARUN enters at some point in this ritual and watches, silently. He then steps closer.*

LANE   Hello.

ARUN   *(stops)* You heard me.

LANE   Ya, about fifty miles from here. How come you're spying on me?

ARUN   I wasn't. I just wanted to look at your dog. Is it dead or asleep?

LANE   Don't know.

> *She gives BLAZE a shake. He wakes and growls at ARUN.*

LANE   Asleep I guess.

> *BLAZE growls again.*

ARUN   Does he bite?

LANE   She.

ARUN   She.

LANE   Sometimes. You mean people, don't you? Does she bite people?

ARUN   Yea.

LANE   That's what I thought you meant. My name's Lane. What's yours?

ARUN   Roon.

LANE   You like this field, Roon?

ARUN   Yea, I like it all right. I come here all the time.

> *LANE turns her head in ARUN's direction.*

LANE   You're not a liar, are you Roon?

ARUN   No.

LANE   I hate liars. You can't trust what they say to you, and if you can't trust what they say, there's hardly any reason to talk to them. It'd be worse than talking to yourself because at least when you talk to yourself you know if you're lying or not. Course, it can get pretty boring talking to yourself. I know. I talk to myself, and it bores me, almost as much as talking to Blaze bores me. Do you talk to yourself?

ARUN   Well–

LANE   I guess that's personal, and my mother tells me all the time not to *pry*, says that's not very polite behaviour, but about the lying. The reason I ask is because *I've* played in this field all last week and the week before that and the one before that and unless you were under a rock or something like that, I didn't notice you.

ARUN   I meant before then. I've been away at camp, but when I'm not at camp, I come here all the time.

LANE   Oh. I just moved into this neighbourhood four weeks ago, so I wouldn't have met you before that. I guess that explains things. My mother says if you're patient eventually, everything gets explained. For instance, you're probably wondering why I've got these cucumbers over my eyes. The reason is because they're cool and on a hot day like this my mother says they're the best protection against sunstroke. I've never had sunstroke, but my mother says that you get *dizzy* and *sick* and it makes you feel *crazy*. That's why I have the cucumbers over my eyes. Now you know.

     Pause.

ARUN   You think she'd bite me if I pet her?

LANE   Blaze or my mother?

ARUN   Blaze.

LANE   Naw. And it wouldn't matter if she did, she's hardly got any teeth left. See?

     LANE pulls up a lip of BLAZE's.

She's an old, old dog. Go ahead.

     ARUN approaches hesitantly. He crouches by BLAZE and lays one hand on her.

ARUN   Good dog. Nice dog. Easy girl.

     He strokes BLAZE gently.

That's a dog. Okay. I like animals. I'd like to have a pet like this, but my father won't let me.

LANE   Is that right? How come?

ARUN   Easy girl. There's a dog. He says they cost too much to feed. He says they *bark* all the time.

LANE   *(cheerfully)* Our dad said the same thing, but it's too late. We already have Blaze, and he can't get rid of her now. Cucumber, Roon? Keep you from going crazy from the heat?

ARUN   Uh, no thanks. Maybe later.

LANE   'Kay.

ARUN   Good Blaze. Easy girl. I think she likes me.

LANE   She's asleep Roon.

ARUN   That's what I mean. She must like me to feel relaxed enough to sleep, don't you think?

LANE   Guess so.

ARUN   I wish we could get a dog. I want to grow up to be a biologist.

LANE   You do? Me too!

ARUN   Really?

LANE   Ya, kind of. I want to be a geologist.

ARUN   That's not the same. A biologist studies animals, a geologist studies rocks.

LANE   I *know*. But they *sound* the same—geologist/biologist—and they're both scientists and studying things and all that and besides I was just trying to be polite, I mean, I've just met you and you're patting my dog and all I know about you is that you like animals and want to be a biologist. What am I *going* to say? "A biologist! Who'd want to be *that*?" That wouldn't be polite. It'd be like spitting in your soup or putting bugs in your bed.

ARUN   Is that why those are there?

LANE   What?

ARUN   Those rocks.

LANE   What about them?

ARUN   Is that why they're there? Because you want to study
         them? Because you want to grow up to be a geologist?

LANE   Oh no. Those are part of this game I made up. See, the
         small *rough* rocks are all one army, and the small
         smooth rocks are another army, and the small rough
         rocks are riding through the forest on their way to the
         castle when suddenly they're ambushed by the small
         smooth rocks. The smooth rocks say, in like their small
         smooth voices, "Where are *you* going?" And the rough
         ones say roughly "To the castle." And the smooth ones
         say "No way." And the rough ones say "Who's going
         to *stop* us?" And the smooth ones say "*We* are!" And
         then they *fight* and get all mixed up and this *big* rock
         which is the king of the castle says "Stop fighting, stop
         fighting!" But they don't, so then I drop the big rock
         on the little rocks and they stop.

                 Pause.

ARUN   And then what?

LANE   And then nothing. That's the end.

ARUN   Don't the small rocks do anything to the big rock?

LANE   No, they can't. He's the *big* rock.

                 Slight pause.

ARUN   Are you *sure* these cucumbers keep you from going
         crazy?

LANE   That's very funny. You're a very funny guy, Roon.
         I like that. You know what? I bet we're in the same
         grade.

ARUN   I'm going into grade four.

LANE   Super. Me too. You're from around here, aren't you?

ARUN   I live five blocks over.

LANE   I bet we're going to the same school.

ARUN   Bridgeway?

LANE   Yup. Is it any good?

ARUN   It's a school.

LANE   Good. I didn't know anyone there before. Now I do. You want a piece of cucumber yet?

ARUN   To put on my eyes?

LANE   No, to eat. Very good if you're thirsty.

ARUN   I have some gum. Want some?

LANE   Sure.

       ARUN tosses her some.

       Can I have some?

ARUN   I tossed it to you.

LANE   Where?

       She feels the ground for it.

ARUN   Beside you.

LANE   Just tell me where.

ARUN   Beside you. *Beside* you! Are you blind?

LANE   Yes.

       ARUN laughs, then stops. Pause.

ARUN   You're kidding. Aren't you?

LANE   No. I'm not. I can't see you and I can't see the gum. Can you hand it to me?

        ARUN hands her the gum.

        Thanks.

ARUN   I didn't know.

LANE   That's okay. Lot's of people don't at first. I mean, there's no law that says I have to have "I am blind" printed on my forehead.

ARUN   I get it! This is one of those dogs that help you get around.

LANE   Blaze? Don't make me laugh. I get around on my own. From my house I can walk here, to Mill's Corner Store, to the school, to the swimming pool, almost anywhere. I've got it all memorized. Mom and Dad just have me take Blaze around for show. Protection, kind of.

        Pause.

ARUN   So, you never could see?

LANE   When I was a baby I could see things if you held them right up here.

        She indicates her nose.

        But it got worse. Now I can only see some light and some dark. Eventually I won't see anything.

ARUN   How come you're going to come to our school? Don't you go to a special school?

LANE   The school for the blind is way far away and I'd have to live in a different city. My parents are going to send me to it when I get to grade seven.

ARUN   How do you read?

LANE   My brother reads my assignments and stuff to me.
I can write.

>*Pause.*

ARUN   How do you get around school?

LANE   I feel my way at first. Eventually I memorize it all.
And Ben, he's my brother, he helps to begin with. *Hey!*
You know, there'll be my brother like I was saying, to
kind of show me around, but he's in grade six and it's
a different grade and all, and also it's a new school to
him too. *You* could give me a hand if you wanted.
I only ask cause we seem to have things in common
like you wanting to be a biologist and me a geologist,
and you liking dogs and not having one and me liking
dogs and having one. That's the only reason, really. So,
what'd'ya think? I'm not trying to pry, I just want to
know.

ARUN   I guess I could take you around.

LANE   Yea?

ARUN   Yea. Why not?

LANE   Excellent! I memorize things *so* quick, you'll be
surprised. *Hey!* Why don't you come home with me?
I can introduce you to my parents.

ARUN   I don't know. It's getting kind of late. I'd have to check
with my folks first.

LANE   We have some other pets you could see. A cat, and a
budgie, a pair of gerbils – Mom has fish but I don't
count them as pets, they're more like scenery or
something.

>*LANE cocks her head.*

Hello? Ben?

>*BEN appears, but reacts in a very aloof manner to
ARUN.*

BEN   Hi. What're you doing here?

LANE   Ben, this is Roon. He's in the same grade as me and goes to the same school, so he can show me around first day!

BEN   That's okay. I guess I can take care of that.

LANE   But he's in the same grade and he said he didn't mind.

         LANE turns her head in the direction of ARUN.

LANE   Roon? This is Ben – my brother I was talking about.

ARUN   Hello.

BEN   *(coolly)* Hi. *(to LANE)* Mom wants you to come home to dinner now.

LANE   I was thinking we could invite Roon for dinner.

BEN   I don't think so. It's already made.

LANE   What is it?

BEN   What does it matter? Spaghetti, I think.

LANE   She could make more.

BEN   I told you, it's made already. Now c'mon.

ARUN   That's all right. I'd have to ask my parents first anyway, and it's late. I should go. Bye.

LANE   Bye. Nice talking to you.

         ARUN starts to leave.

     Where do you live?

ARUN   Last house on Fifth street, toward the school.

LANE   Maybe I'll call on you before school starts.

ARUN   Okay.

LANE   See ya!

>   *ARUN goes. LANE turns furiously on her brother,*
>   *finds his sleeve and then hits him on the chest.*

Why were you so *mean* to him? He's the first friend
I've made here!

BEN   We would have got in trouble if we'd brought him
home.

LANE   Why?

BEN   Because he's Indian. Like from India.

LANE   Him?

BEN   Yea.

>   *Pause.*

LANE   Oh.

>   *Pause.*

BEN   We better go. Mom's waiting.

>   *They start to go.*

LANE   You're sure, hey?

BEN   Definitely Indian.

LANE   Blaze, come.

>   *BLAZE joins LANE and BEN, and together they exit.*

SCENE TWO

LANE   So, that's what happened in the field that day, and that's how I met Roon and how we left each other.

The next time in the field was a couple days later on the weekend before school. One moment it was summer, and the next it was like fall. A couple of days of fog, rain and wind, and the leaves started falling. Then there's frost on the grass and birds are passing overhead, going somewhere warmer, flying away, away, far away.

This time the field is like this: frosty, smelling of wet and mould. And there's one bird in a tree, calling out.

The puppeteer makes a bird sound.

And me, I'm in the field listening to that one bird all on its own, and flying a kite.

With that, she sends up a kite, which swoops over the heads of the audience, manipulated by the same puppeteer.

Whenever the wind blows strong, the kite tugs and pulls at my arms, and when it's soft, the kite starts to droop and drop and I have to wind up real quick on my spool of string.

ARUN enters.

Hello?

ARUN   Hello.

LANE   Oh, its you.

ARUN   Yea.

He looks up at the kite.

You haven't come by.

LANE	No, there's been a lot going on.
ARUN	Yea?
LANE	Yea.
ARUN	Like what?
LANE	Just stuff.
ARUN	Blaze is asleep.
LANE	She gets bored when I mess around with a kite for too long.
ARUN	Can I pat her again?
LANE	Be my guest.

ARUN crouches by BLAZE.

ARUN	Good girl. Easy girl. That's a girl.

BLAZE raises her head.

She woke up!

LANE	It's not often she gets attention like that. She probably likes it.
	Just then a real strong gust of wind blew up, hard as nails and cold. I grabbed the kite string tight to keep it from ripping out of my hands–
ARUN	Wow, some wind, hey?
LANE	–and then just as suddenly the wind stopped, and the kite came tumbling back at me.

BLAZE rises and barks at the kite.

Quiet Blaze. Quiet! Sit girl!

ARUN	What's the matter with her?

LANE	Whenever the kite starts coming down like that she gets upset – she thinks it's attacking me or whatever. Crazy, hey?
ARUN	How come your brother doesn't like me?
LANE	Who says he doesn't?
ARUN	It doesn't seem like he does.
LANE	Well, he's funny in some ways. What's Roon short for?
ARUN	Arun. My full name is Arun Sood.
LANE	What kind of name is that?
ARUN	Indian. My parents came from Delhi, in India. Good Blaze. Easy girl.

       Pause.

LANE	I didn't know.
ARUN	Well, it's like you said. There's no law says I've got to wear a big sign saying what I am.
LANE	I couldn't read it anyway. So, do you come from a big family?
ARUN	No, just me, my mother, father and older sister. Four.
LANE	Just four, hey? That's the same as us. You don't have any relatives staying with you?
ARUN	No. You?
LANE	Uh uh. What's your father do?
ARUN	He's an accountant. Your dad?
LANE	A mechanic.
ARUN	Good Blaze. That's a dog.

LANE   You ever fly a kite?

ARUN   No.

LANE   Want to?

ARUN   Sure.

> *They exchange the string carefully, from one hand to the other.*

LANE   Just keep the line tight, that's the trick.

ARUN   It's way, way up there.

LANE   Yea.

> *ARUN operates the kite.*

You know how Blaze barked when the kite started coming down?

ARUN   Yea?

LANE   My brother's kinda' the same way. He watches out for me, and if he feels I'm threatened or anything, well.... He's always watching. You know?

ARUN   What do you mean? What'd he feel threatened by? Lane?

> *Pause.*

LANE   I don't care what my dad says. He's wrong.

ARUN   Now what are you talking about?

LANE   Well, he hasn't said anything about *you* really. He says it about Indians, you know? He says they come over here and get jobs and then bring all their family over, and they can barely speak our language and talk with an accent and eat nothing but curry and oh... all kinds of stuff. But you're not like that. I asked Ben how you were dressed and he said you dressed just normal, and

I can't hear any accent, and you haven't got a big family or anything, so he's gotta' be wrong.

ARUN So that's why you didn't come over.

>   *Pause.*

I eat curry all the time, I like it. It's a spice, like ketchup, or pepper or...

My father and mother both came over from India fifteen years ago. They've been here longer than you or me have been alive.

My mother still wears a sari sometimes. It's like a robe. And they talk with a different accent because they've talked in another language most of their lives, but they're still really good people, and they're still my parents, and if you think that's funny...

>   *He hands the kite string back to LANE and leaves.*

LANE Roon? Roon?

And then suddenly a strong gust blew up outta' nowhere and snatched the string out of my hand.

Hey!

>   *The kite flies off, as the puppeteer takes it off stage. BEN enters.*

BEN Lane? Mom just gave me some money and told me to get you and we could go buy a few things for school. I've been doing some yard work, so she even gave me a bit extra to get a pop or something. Let's go. Lane? What's the matter?

LANE I lost my kite.

SCENE THREE

LANE   A week later, suddenly we're back to summer again, the end of summer. Leaves drooping, the weather hot and dry and lazy feeling. School has started, we've been at it a week, and it's soooo different from the school we were used to. Bigger, way more modern, more kids, more teachers, more classrooms, more *everything*.

But this is the weekend and we're back in the field again. Nothing much else to do.

Ben? Get up. Get up, Ben.

BEN   No.

LANE   Get up, let's do something.

BEN   I don't feel like getting up.

LANE   Let's play hide and seek.

BEN   I don't feel like playing hide and seek.

LANE   Well what do you feel like playing?

BEN   I feel like playing "I lie here and you play hide and seek on your own."

LANE   That's no good.

BEN   No good for you, maybe. Plenty good for me.

LANE   Quit being so depressing. You've been depressing ever since school started last Monday.

BEN   I've been depressing since Monday because things have *been* depressing since Monday. It's not the same as school back home. Everyone here's already got friends. Everything's so big.

LANE   I know. I *hate* finding my way around school. There's
          so many classrooms and hallways and they're always
          filled with kids going in the other direction. I haven't
          made any friends either. All the kids look at me like
          I was a freak.

BEN   How do *you* know how they look at you?

LANE   I can tell.

BEN   You cannot.

LANE   Can.

BEN   Cannot.

LANE   Can.

BEN   You do *not* know how they're looking at you. *I* know
          how they're looking at you. You don't, end of story.

LANE   Well, tell me then, Mr. Know-it-all, do the kids, or do
          they not, when I am walking down the hallway turn
          and look at me like I had a *tail*, or had a string of drool
          trailing from my mouth? Well?

BEN   Some of them, maybe. Some of the time.

LANE   Well.

BEN   I wish we'd move back home.

LANE   We can't. Dad's got his job here. We'll be here for
          years, maybe billions of years.

          You know who's got lots of friends?

BEN   Who?

LANE   Roon.

BEN   Yea?

LANE   He's really popular. He's good in gym class and smart too.

BEN   That right?

LANE   Uh huh.

BEN   He's got a sister in my grade. She's about the same. She doesn't talk to me, neither do her friends. Her brother must've said something to her.

LANE   I guess. You know, I don't see what the big deal is about them? Where did Dad get all this stuff, anyway?

BEN   Dunno.

LANE   Were there any Indians in our town?

BEN   I never saw any. He must've seen some somewhere though.

LANE   Maybe, but he never saw Roon or his sister.

BEN   No.

LANE   Even if they had accents and all that, they'd still be the same people, wouldn't they?

BEN   I guess. Maybe. It doesn't matter though. Dad wouldn't understand. All I know is that those two hate our guts, and all their friends hate our guts and we haven't even been in school two weeks. Just think how many people will hate our guts by *Christmas*. Maybe a couple'a hundred. I've never had that many people hate my guts. I think that's more than there was in our whole school back home. *Then* we'll go on to Junior High, where even *more* people will hate our guts.

LANE   *(glumly)* Yea.

        That is, they'll hate *your* guts. I'll be in blind school.

BEN   That's right. I'll be alone when they're all hating my guts. And then, *High School*.

LANE   Let's play hide and seek. It'll cheer you up.

BEN   All right, all right. Cover your ears.

> *LANE covers her ears and counts to ten–*

LANE   One, two, three, four, five, six…

> *–while BEN moves to another location and crouches, perfectly still.*

LANE   …seven, eight, nine, ten.

> *She uncovers her ears, and listens for BEN. She sweeps the ground near her.*

Okay. Where are you?

> *BEN continues to stay perfectly still.*

Make a sound.

> *Pause.*

Make a sound, Ben!

> *BEN snaps his fingers. LANE starts moving toward the sound. She listens and moves closer and closer. Suddenly there is a noise from another direction. It's ARUN.*

Who's that?

ARUN   Me.

LANE   What are you doing here?

ARUN   I have as much right to be here as you. More. I was here first. I talked with my Dad the other day and asked him what I should do if I met people who didn't like us because of what we are and he said I should

just ignore them, but I shouldn't be afraid to go
wherever I wanted even if they're there, because
I have my rights. So, I'm here because I've got a
right to be here.

BEN   So do we.

ARUN   I never said you didn't. But I'm not going to be chased
out of here because you don't like Indians.

LANE   Fine.

ARUN   Fine.

> *ARUN tosses a ball and catches it in a glove.*

LANE   Hide somewhere else, Ben.

> *He moves and she counts.*

One, two, three, four, five, six... I never said I hated
Indians.

ARUN   Yea.

LANE   I did not. I said my father didn't like them, and I was
halfway to apologizing anyway when you left me
standing there like a monkey and I lost my kite.

BEN   That kite was a present too.

LANE   Ben! I thought you were hiding!

BEN   I didn't know we were still playing the game.

ARUN   You didn't apologize. You made fun of my parents.
You said they talk funny.

LANE   I never said they talk funny, *you* said they talk funny.
I've never heard your parents.

ARUN   I said they talk *different* and it's people like you who
find it funny.

LANE   Funny, different, it's the same thing.

ARUN   Oh yea?

LANE   Yea.

ARUN   Then I guess you don't mind when people laugh at you cause you walk into a door or end up in the wrong classroom at school?

> *Pause. LANE refuses to admit the difference.*

BEN   Sure there's a difference. I know it, and so do you Lane. I've gotten into fights with kids who laughed at you, and you know that's because there's a big difference.

I don't hate you. I don't know what I feel about you, really, cause my Dad's kind of got his own opinions. But I hardly know you, and you can't hate someone you don't know. That'd be crazy.

That's why I don't get why your sister hates me. We've hardly met. She doesn't know what I'm like.

ARUN   I don't know what you're talking about.

BEN   Don't tell me you haven't said anything about me to your sister.

ARUN   I haven't said a thing about you to anyone. Even when I was talking to my father I never mentioned your names. I thought it was my business.

BEN   Then why does she hate me?

ARUN   I don't know. Does she? I haven't heard anything about you. I don't think she even knows you to put a name to. I mean, it's only been a week of school.

BEN   You haven't said anything?

ARUN   No.

Pause.

I brought a bone for Blaze. I thought "Blaze hasn't done anything. Why should she suffer?" Where is she?

LANE   I don't know. Somewhere round here. Blaze? Do you see her, Ben?

BEN   Uh uh.

LANE   Blaze?

BEN   Blaze?

ARUN   Blaze?

LANE   That's weird, I haven't heard her in the past fifteen minutes or so.

BEN   Me neither.

ARUN   Did she go home, maybe?

BEN   Naw. She sticks pretty close to Lane. Here Blaze! She'll go maybe a hundred feet away, but she always comes back. Blaze? This is *so* weird.

ARUN   Maybe she got as far as the street and got picked up by the dog catcher?

LANE   Uh uh. She'd have barked. I'd have heard. Bla-aze!

They listen.

I wonder if she hurt herself or something. Let's divide up and search. I'll check over there by the bushes.

ARUN   I'll check over by the spruce trees and the shack.

BEN   I'll check the poplars.

They search.

Blaze?

LANE   Blaze?

ARUN   Blaze?

LANE   Anything?

BEN   No. Nothing. What about the shack, anything over there?

ARUN   No.

LANE   Wait, shh. Quiet. I hear something. It sounds funny–

> *BEN looks over at LANE and starts to approach her.*

BEN   What do you mean?

LANE   Like she was, underground, or something…. In there, in the bushes. I can hear something, and I can feel… something… wooden…

> *LANE shoves through the bushes, BEN sees something and comes running. At the same time, as LANE pushes through the bushes, the bushes themselves are transformed into the opening of a well.*

BEN   Stand back! There's a hole! Ahhh–

> *BEN falls into the well.*

LANE   Ben! Ben!

ARUN   Stand back! Don't go any closer.

> *BEN has disappeared down into the well.*

LANE   What's happened? Tell me what's happened?

ARUN   He's fallen into, something–

LANE   What?

ARUN   –looks like an old, boarded-up well. It's all grown over and stuff.

ARUN pulls some of the bush material aside.

LANE   Ben? Ben, are you all right? Can you see him?

ARUN   I can't get close enough to look down, it's crumbling around the edges.

LANE   Get on your belly and crawl up, I'll hold your feet.

ARUN   Okay.

                 You'll hold on, right?

LANE   I've got you.

> *ARUN lies down, LANE holds his feet. ARUN looks down into the well.*

ARUN   It's dark. I can't make out... no.... There he is! And Blaze too! Ben?

LANE   Ben? Ben, are you okay?

BEN   I'm okay. I think I'm okay. I must've blacked out or something when I fell. I woke up and found out I'm all covered with mud, and the walls around me are slimy. And when I touch the walls, whole chunks come off in my hands. Where am I? What is this?

ARUN   It's an old well. All the old houses around here used to have them. Most people covered them up eventually, but the cover on this one must've rotted and Blaze must've broken through. I heard of something like this happening a year ago to a kid a couple blocks over.

LANE   Can you get out?

BEN   There's nothing to hang onto. And the walls keep crumbling.

LANE   Can you help him out?

ARUN   He's too far down. I can't reach him.

LANE   Can you reach up, Ben?

BEN   I'm too far down.

        Pause.

        It's kinda' scary down here.

LANE   Maybe you better get some help.

ARUN   I don't know if we should leave him.

LANE   I'll stay. You go get someone.

ARUN   All right.

        To LANE as he leaves:

        Stay away from the edge.

LANE   Yea.

        Long pause.

        Whew, huh?

BEN   What?

LANE   I said "whew." I though we'd lost you for sure.

BEN   Me too.

        Pause.

LANE   Watch out for that last step, hey?

        They both laugh nervously.

BEN   Ah!

LANE   What is it?

BEN   Nothing. Just some mud from the sides slid down on
        me. It's all right. Just a little creepy is all.

You know what, Lane?

LANE   What?

BEN   I don't think the walls to this thing are so strong anymore. Ah!

LANE   What?

BEN   Some more just came down.

LANE   Are you all right? Ben? Ben?

BEN   Stay away from the edge! When you come close all kinds of muck falls in from the sides.

You don't think this thing's going to fall in on me, do you?

LANE   No. Roon will be back with help any time now. You'll see. Just sit tight.

BEN   Don't go away.

LANE   I'm not going away.

Pause.

Ben?

BEN   Yea?

LANE   You sitting tight?

BEN   Yea.

Pause.

LANE   Ben?

BEN   Yea?

LANE   You know that knife of yours with the fish scaling attachment?

BEN   Yea.

LANE   You know how you couldn't find it?

BEN   Yea?

LANE   I took it.

BEN   You know what?

LANE   What?

BEN   If I get outta" here, you can keep it.

LANE   I hear something. Someone's coming. Arun?

>   *ARUN enters.*

>   Did you find someone? I don't hear anybody?

ARUN   Not exactly.

LANE   What do you mean?

ARUN   I brought back this dead tree–

LANE   A dead tree?

ARUN   –from over there in the poplars. I think it's long enough. If we don't touch the sides of the well, lower it down to him... he should be able to climb out.

LANE   Don't you think you should've got some help?

ARUN   Maybe, but I was worried about the well. It's not so sturdy, right? Anyway, I think this will do the trick. Can you climb out?

BEN   I don't know. Is the tree strong enough?

ARUN   I don't know. Think so. Okay, I'm going to start lowering it, tell me if it's going down straight because I don't want to touch the walls.

Pause.

BEN   Careful!

ARUN   I'm trying.

LANE   What about Blaze?

BEN   I'll tie her up in my jacket and put her around my neck. If you lower it just a bit more, I can grab the tip and pull it down.

There. The thing is on the bottom.

ARUN   Now, we can rest the top part against this bush branch and Lane, if you can help me hold it in place so it doesn't spin while he's climbing up.

LANE   Where is it?

ARUN   Here. Hold tight.

LANE   I will.

BEN   Can I climb up?

ARUN   Go ahead.

BEN steps onto the tree.

BEN   Oooh. It's... not a *big* tree, is it? Not very, strong.

ARUN   I didn't want a *big* tree. A big tree wouldn't fit.

BEN   I wanted a tree that'll hold me.

ARUN   It's the only tree I could find.

BEN   I just hope it doesn't break.

ARUN   Me too.

LANE   Just *climb* will you, Ben?

BEN   Okay.

            He climbs.

ARUN   Almost there. Lane, you hold on. I'll take his hand.

            Reach out.

BEN   Got me?

ARUN   Ya, I got you. Okay, jump away from it.

            BEN jumps and is out and safe.

LANE   And then we heard...

**BEN,
LANE &
ARUN**   KA-THUMP!

            The three children are knocked down.

LANE   ...and I felt this huge "whoooosh" and felt a great
            smack of cold, wet air knock me off my feet, and then
            heard this other sound like a bed collapsing—only a
            hundred times louder—and dust and grass and mud
            and bits of twigs all came flying up toward us.

            What's that?

BEN   The hole and the planking and everything's
            disappeared into this muddy dent in the ground. It's
            gone, the hole's gone. I guess the well's collapsed.

            Pause.

ARUN   That's what happened to the kid who fell into that
            well last year. He didn't get out.

            Pause.

BEN   I guess it's a good thing you got that tree then.

            Whoa, I've never felt so happy to be bruised, wet
            and slimy.

LANE   You're not hurt too bad?

BEN   I'm a bit shook up. Think I've got a cut on my head,
          do I?

          LANE runs a hand over his face.

BEN   Ow.

LANE   Feels like.

ARUN   And what about the dog? How are you? Here's a bone
          I brought for you.

BEN   How would you like to take Blaze home? I mean to
          our home.

ARUN   I don't know.

BEN   I've got to tell my father what happened. I mean, he's
          going to see *something's* happened, and I think he
          might like to meet you. He should meet you. If you
          want to come.

          Slight pause.

ARUN   Could I carry Blaze?

LANE   I think she might like that after such a long fall. Up
          Blaze.

          ARUN picks up BLAZE.

ARUN   Thanks. Good dog. That's a girl.

          ARUN, BLAZE and BEN exit.

LANE   We got home, told Dad and Mom about the field and
          what'd happened. Mom cried. Dad phoned the mayor,
          city works came by and put up a big "Danger. No
          Trespassing" sign. Later a city crew drove up with
          some big machines and land movers and they totally
          levelled the field, which seemed kinda' drastic to me,
          but I guess it was to be expected. So. That was the end
          of the field, grass, trees, shack, well, and everything.

Dad was surprised to hear our story and meet Roon. Surprised at the kind of guy Roon was. Still is. We, Ben and Roon and I, hang out together all the time now.

But I guess that's another story.

LANE begins to exit.

Guys! Wait up!

She exits. Lights fade.

The end.

Mouse

(l to r) Matthew Kennedy, Cam Ascroft, Shannon Anderson, Kathy Fraser.
Photo by Trudie Lee.

Mouse was first produced by Quest Theatr, touring Alberta, fall 2001, with the following cast and crew:

BOWEY / SAGE   Matthew Kennedy
FATHER / COACH / SAGE   Cam Ascroft
MAMA / TEACHER / SAGE   Shannon Anderson
JESSE (JOSH)   Kathy Fraser

Directed by Duval Lang
Set, Costumes and Lighting designed by Scott Reid
Stage Managed by Marcia Januska
Assistant Director: Bruce Horak
Composer: David Rhymer

CHARACTERS

JOSH
A young mouse.

BOWEY
Another young mouse, a friend to the previous mouse.

MAMA
Josh's mother, a mouse.

FATHER
Josh's father, a mouse.

BROTHER
A variety of mice, all brothers to Josh.

TEACHER MOUSE
A learned adult mouse.

COACH
The physical education specializing mouse.

SAGE
A wise mouse.

Mice, each and every one. However the entire cast can be portrayed by four human actors.

ACT ONE

It is dark and terribly quiet. As our eyes gradually adjust to the gloom, we become aware of the sounds associated with deep sleep: sighs, groans, the occasional snore and heavy, slow, rhythmic breathing. Then... an odd sound is heard, like wind blowing softly, and the far-away screeching of car wheels. JOSH enters the stage from outside the cage. He looks at the mice sleeping, and takes out a set of mouse ears, a mouse nose, and a thin, long mouse tail. He puts them on, and joins the mice on stage.

Then suddenly, lights snap on!

At once we become aware of the setting, which in this case is the confines of an enormous cage for mice. Wood chips and shredded cardboard cover the floor. A water applicator is thrust out on the side of the cage, as is a small food bin filled with seeds. A running-wheel is situated in the corner, and up along the back wall are a number of brightly-coloured plastic tunnels that zig-zag off in a variety of directions.

FATHER   Ah!

Shrieking with terror at the onset of light, the FATHER rises up out of the wood shavings, and then, realizing what time it is, he shrieks again.

Ah!

He leaps from his soft bed of wood chips and ripped cardboard. Startled by the cries of her husband, MAMA awakens as well and leaps out of her wood chips.

MAMA   Ah!

> *JOSH sits straight up from his bed of wood chips, startled and alarmed by the fuss his parents are making. All of these mice, and any subsequent ones, have big mouse ears, large mouse noses and thin, long mouse tails. Beyond that, they appear to be dressed just as you or I – which is to say, casually.*
>
> *One should also say that all the mice brothers look almost exactly alike, because they are played by the same actor.*

JOSH   Ah!

FATHER   I'm gonna' be late! I'm gonna' be late!

> *Both MAMA and FATHER race about in frantic circles. JOSH continues to sit, blinking.*

MAMA   Get up. Get up. The lab lights have come on.

> *She races around the cage in the opposite direction from FATHER, throwing around every bit as much sawdust and debris as he does.*

MAMA   You'll–

FATHER   I'll–

BOTH   –be late.

> *Music begins here and runs throughout this next "getting up" portion, not only under the dialogue which is sung, but that which is spoken as well.*

MAMA   *(singing)* Get up, get up,
Everyone in the cage get up.
It's time to rise and shine
And shake a leg.

(spoken) I've made some breakfast. Have a
pumpkin seed.

> *She throws FATHER a pumpkin seed.*

FATHER   No time.

              He throws it back.

MAMA   You need something.

              She throws it back.

FATHER   Not *now*.

              He throws it back.

MAMA   For goodness sake, at *least* have a drink from the
              water applicator.

              *FATHER races to the water applicator and drinks
              and gargles loudly. JOSH rises from his wood
              chips looking very sleepy.*

JOSH   I'm up. It's not necessary to make any more
              noise.

FATHER   (*singing*) Get up, get up
              There are things we have to do, get up.
              It's time to rise and shine
              And shake a leg – do I look all right?

MAMA   Straighten your hair.
              (*to JOSH*) Have you washed?

              She begins to lick vigorously behind his ears.

JOSH   Ma!

              (*singing*) Get up, Get up,
              Every morning it's the same "Get up"
              I need to rise and shine and shake a leg – what's
              that *mean*?

              *FATHER goes to the wheel and runs on it.
              BROTHER jumps up out of the shavings.*

BROTHER   Oh-my-gosh, look at the time. *Look* at the time.

JOSH   Dad!

FATHER   What?

JOSH   You're running in the same spot. That can't be very productive.

FATHER   Right. Thanks.

        He steps off the wheel.

        How do I look?

MAMA   Great.

        MAMA and FATHER quickly rub noses.

FATHER   Bye.

ALL   *(singing)* Get a move on,
There's no time now,
You have got to,
Rise and shine now,
Shake a leg and
Greet the day now,
Can't you see that,
You can't stay now,

BROTHER   Can I have some lunch to take with me?

ALL   Put your hat on,
Tie your shoe lace,
You have got to,
Join the rat race,

FATHER   Come on. We're going to be late for the Maze.

ALL   Keep on moving,
Keep on moving,
Don't look back now
Keep on moving,
Keep your chin up,
Set your mind straight,
You might keep up,
If you're not late.

MAMA   Here's a pumpkin seed.

                *BROTHER takes the seed and races off through
                the tunnels. JOSH and MAMA are left in the
                relative calm aftermath of the departure.*

JOSH &
MAMA   Get up, get up,
                Next day it'll be just the same
                Just a new day with another name,
                So rise and shine and play the game,
                Get up.

JOSH   *Who* is he again?

MAMA   Your *brother*.

JOSH   Right. Which one?

MAMA   Number 22. Lewis.

JOSH   Right.

                Another BROTHER enters.

BROTHER   Have they left already?

MAMA   Yes.

BROTHER   Without me?

MAMA   They're gone.

BROTHER   Have you got something packed for me?

MAMA   A sunflower seed is the best I could do, we slept
                in.

BROTHER   Thanks.

                This BROTHER races off as well.

JOSH   Which is he?

MAMA	Josh. That's Brother 14. Langston. Now you better get on your way.
JOSH	Bye.
MAMA	Have you got everything you need?
JOSH	I'm a *mouse*, Mom. What do I need?
MAMA	Get going.
JOSH	Goodbye.
MAMA	Bye.

JOSH and MAMA rub noses, JOSH exits for school and is met up by his best friend, BOWEY.

BOWEY	Hey.
JOSH	Hi.

They stop long enough to quickly perform their special, rather complicated, handshake. They do this each time they greet, and it always ends with these next three lines:

JOSH & BOWEY	Smooooth.
BOWEY	Going to be a good day?
JOSH	Going to be a great day.
BOWEY	We're late.
JOSH	Of course we are.

They run in circles.

BOWEY	Whew. We're here.
TEACHER	Okay class. Find your places.

The mice take their places.

TEACHER   Take your papers.

Everyone takes their papers.

TEACHER   Has everyone got their papers?

A number of mice heads pop up from the sawdust – the other students.

STUDENTS   Yes, teacher.

JOSH   *(whispering)* I don't have my papers.

BOWEY   *(whispering)* What do you mean you don't have your papers?

JOSH   *(whispering)* I don't have my papers.

BOWEY   *(whispering)* What did you do with them?

JOSH   *(whispering)* I must've forgot them.

TEACHER   What's that whispering about?

JOSH &
BOWEY   Nothing.

BOWEY   How could you forget?

JOSH   *(whispering)* I have other things on my mind.

BOWEY   *(whispering)* What "other things?"

JOSH   *(whispering)* Other "other things." Lend me your paper.

BOWEY   *(whispering)* No.

JOSH   *(whispering)* C'mon.

TEACHER   Is everyone ready?

BOWEY   *(whispering)* What if I get caught?

JOSH   *(whispering)* You won't get caught.

BOWEY   Just *one*.

TEACHER   Excuse me?

BOWEY   Nothing. *(whispering to JOSH)* Just *one*.

JOSH   *(whispering)* C'mon. A few.

BOWEY   *(whispering) Here.*

TEACHER   Josh! Bowie! Have you got your papers?

BOTH   Yes!

TEACHER   Hm. I smell a rat. Let me see.

BOWEY   Here.

TEACHER   And yours?

JOSH   Here.

> *She inspects the papers, in a typically mouse fashion. Smelling them up and down. They appear to be in order. She counts them.*

TEACHER   One, two, four, five, six–

JOSH   Hey! Didn't you forget something?

> *He glances about, but no one seems to have noticed.*

TEACHER   Pardon me?

JOSH   But. Didn't anyone–

> *BOWEY stares back at him.*

TEACHER   That'll do. Everyone – papers ready? You may
             begin.

                         They begin furiously shredding papers with their
                         teeth. Paper flies in all directions. Music plays to
                         indicate the passage of time.

JOSH &
BOWEY   Rip, rip, rip, rip
            Rip, rip, rip, rip
            Take a stack and
            Keep on ripping.

JOSH   How can we do this every day?

BOWEY   Sh.

ALL   Keep on shredding
            Keep on shredding
            No distractions
            Keep on shredding

JOSH   Don't you feel… ridiculous?

BOWEY   Actually, I kinda' enjoy it.

            There is nothing
            Like the power
            Of shredding pages
            By the hour

TEACHER   Use your paws or
            Use your teeth
            Above your head
            Or underneath.

BOWEY   First you rip it
            Then you spike it.

JOSH   I don't get it.

BOWEY   I quite like it.

> Shred the paper
> Take some more
> Watch the scraps pile
> on the floor.

ALL

> Shred the paper
> Shred the paper
> Faster, faster
> Shred the paper
> Don't ask questions
> Of your neighbour
> Shred the paper
> Shred the paper

JOSH

> It just makes me
> Want to throw up

TEACHER

> It will make sense
> When you grow up

> *By the end they have enormous piles of shredded paper beside them.*

TEACHER

And – papers down. Bowey – very good. Josh – a little disappointing. Class dismissed.

> *The class bell rings. The day is done. BOWEY and JOSH head back home.*

BOWEY

Whoa. That was brutal.

JOSH

It's insane.

BOWEY

Ya, no kidding.

JOSH

I mean, what's the point?

BOWEY

(laughs) As if there's got to be a point to shred paper.

JOSH

Tell me why we do it again.

BOWEY

To prepare of course.

JOSH	For the maze.
BOWEY	Right.
JOSH	And why do we run the maze?

> *BOWEY just laughs at this.*

There are times when I don't think I'll ever be ready for it.

BOWEY	Right.
JOSH	I'm serious.
BOWEY	"I'm serious."

> *BOWEY gives JOSH an affectionate punch.*

You crack me up.

JOSH	What's so funny about that?
BOWEY	You're always saying stuff like that. Like every-thing's "serious."
JOSH	*(simply)* It is.
BOWEY	There you go again! "It is." Ba ba ba ba!

> *The first four dramatic notes of Beethoven's Fifth.*

Lighten up. I'll see you tomorrow.

JOSH	Ya, I guess.
BOWEY	"Ya, I guess." Oh boy.

> *They perform their special handshake ending with:*

JOSH & **BOWEY**	Smooooth.
BOWEY	Hey, what's it going to be tomorrow?

JOSH   Going to be a great day.

BOWEY   See ya.

     BOWEY exits.

JOSH   *(to himself)* "Lighten up." How?

     JOSH returns home.

MAMA   Josh, you're home.

FATHER   What took you so long?

JOSH   We took the blue tunnel.

FATHER   Well hurry up and join us for supper.

     JOSH comes to join the others.

MAMA   Did you wash your hands?

     JOSH halts and quickly licks his hands.

     What will it be?

JOSH   Pumpkin, I guess.

     She gives him a seed. He sits down to supper along with his mouse family. Everyone nibbles furiously on the enormous seeds as they talk, and then fling the seed husks over their shoulders when they're done with them.

FATHER   And I'll take another pumpkin seed as well.

BROTHER   Me too.

FATHER   The seed is *very* good tonight. Very tender.

BROTHER   And flavourful.

FATHER   And moist.

BROTHER	Without losing any crispness in the shell on the outside.
MAMA	Thank you.
JOSH	Can I ask a question?
FATHER	"Can I ask a question?"
BROTHER	You're *always* asking questions.
FATHER	Ask *anything* you want. Anything you want. How are you going to learn if you don't ask?
JOSH	Why do we run the maze?
	Beat.
FATHER	What do you mean?
JOSH	I mean, why do we do it?
FATHER	That's an… unusual question.
BROTHER	It's what lab mice *do*.
JOSH	But. What do you *do* in the maze?
FATHER	What do you do?
BROTHER	Don't you know?
FATHER	You find your way through.
BROTHER	Through to the other end.
FATHER	From the beginning to the end.
BROTHER	From one end to the other.
FATHER	And then back.
JOSH	But. While you're in there. Going from, one end to the other. What?

FATHER   You – try to figure things out. You – try to find
                the right route.

BROTHER   You – look back at the way you've come, look
                ahead to the way you're going.

FATHER   And there are different degrees of difficulty,
                depending upon the maze. Pass me a food pellet.

BROTHER   Pass me a sunflower seed. The yellow maze is
                your level-one maze, it's the easiest to find your
                way through.

FATHER   And then there's your purple maze, it's the next
                level up. It's a higher degree of difficulty.

BROTHER   And then there's your red maze.

FATHER   The most difficult.

BROTHER   There are blind alleyways.

FATHER   Dead ends.

BROTHER   Water traps.

FATHER   There are mice who have gone in there, and
                never come out.

                Beat.

JOSH   And the point of running it is?

BROTHER &
FATHER   To find the cheese of course.

FATHER   Although it varies. Sometimes it's *cheese*.

BROTHER   Sometimes it's seeds.

FATHER   Sometimes, if you're *very* lucky it's peanut butter.

FATHER, MOTHER & BROTHER	Peanut butter. Yummm.
BROTHER	Sometimes, though, there's the *(twitches)* shock instead.
FATHER	I hate the *(twitches)* shock worse than anything. I lit up like the lighting filament once when I ran down that one wrong tunnel.
BROTHER	But don't you worry, you'll be ready when your time comes.
FATHER	You won't have to run the maze until you're completely grown up.
BROTHER	Which for mice is a good, oh, four to six weeks.
	Blackout.
FATHER	Oh. There go the lab lights. Time for bed.
MAMA	I thought that was particularly beautiful, didn't you?
FATHER	Yes, the dimming of the lighting filament was very colorful tonight.
MAMA	The way it winked out. Almost, *poetic*, really.
FATHER	Gorgeous.
	Night.
MAMA	Night.
BROTHER	Night.
JOSH	Ma?
MAMA	Yes?
JOSH	Why do we do this?

MAMA What dear?

JOSH All of this.

MAMA Oh *you*. You and your questions. You just need some sleep.

> *She ruffles his head, then licks his hair to flatten an upright tuft.*

JOSH Ma!

> *She scurries off. In the darkness, one hears the sounds of sleep in the lab. The resonant, rich, harmony of several individuals snoring all together.*
>
> *The snoring slowly fades out and one becomes more aware of another sound. It's like wind blowing, or perhaps breathing. Or maybe like cars rushing past in traffic.*
>
> *JOSH sits up.*

What's that?

> *The sound rises in volume.*

Hello? What's going on?

> *The sound becomes even louder.*

What *is* that?

> *JOSH dives back into his wood shavings. And then all at once – lights! And with lights comes the usual confusion.*

FATHER Ah!

> *Shrieking with terror the FATHER sits up, and then, realizing what time it is, he shrieks again.*

Ah!

He leaps from his bed of wood chips and ripped cardboard. Startled by the cries of her husband, MAMA awakens as well, and leaps out of the wood chips.

MAMA   Ah!

JOSH sits straight up from his bed of wood chips, startled and alarmed.

JOSH   Oh no, not again.

FATHER   I'm gonna' be late! I'm gonna' be late!

Both MAMA and FATHER race about in frantic circles. One of the mouse brothers rises up shrieking and races off like a bullet to the maze without saying a word to anyone. JOSH continues to sit, blinking.

MAMA   Get up. Get up. The lab lights have come on.

She races around the cage in the opposite direction from FATHER, throwing around every bit as much sawdust and debris as he does.

MAMA   You'll–

FATHER   I'll–

BOTH   –be late.

MAMA   Come on, get up. I've made some breakfast. Have a pumpkin seed.

She throws him a pumpkin seed.

FATHER   No time.

He throws it back.

MAMA   Or a food pellet.

FATHER	Not now.
MAMA	At *least* have a drink from the water applicator.

> *FATHER races to the water applicator and drinks and gargles loudly. JOSH rises from his wood chips looking very sleepy.*

JOSH	I'm up. Rest easy everyone. The noise has worked again.
MAMA	Have you washed?

> *She begins to vigorously lick behind his ears.*

JOSH	Ma! Stop with the licking, *please*.

> *FATHER goes to the wheel and runs on it. BROTHER jumps up out of the shavings.*

BROTHER	Oh-my-gosh, look at the time.
JOSH	Dad!
FATHER	What?
JOSH	You're running in the *same* spot.
FATHER	Right. Thanks.

> *He gets off the wheel.*

How do I look?

MAMA	Great.

> *MAMA and FATHER quickly rub noses.*

FATHER	Bye.
BROTHER	Can I have some lunch to take with me?
FATHER	Come on. We're going to be late for the Maze.

MAMA   Here's a pumpkin seed.

                *BROTHER takes the seed and races off through
                the tunnels. JOSH and MAMA are left in the
                relative calm aftermath of the departure.*

JOSH   Who is he again?

MAMA   Your *brother.*

JOSH   Right. Which one?

MAMA   Number 26. Linus.

JOSH   Right.

                And *how* can you tell?

MAMA   Oh *you.* You think a mother doesn't know how to
                tell her sons apart?

                *She pinches his cheek as another BROTHER
                enters.*

BROTHER   Have they left already?

MAMA   Yes.

BROTHER   Have you got something packed for me?

MAMA   A sunflower seed is the best I could do, we slept
                in.

BROTHER   Thanks.

                This BROTHER races off as well.

JOSH   Which?

MAMA   Brother 14. Lawrence.

                She pushes JOSH out the door.

                Better get going.

> *Out he goes. He encounters BOWEY and they*
> *perform their special handshake, ending with:*

JOSH &
BOWEY   Smoooth.

BOWEY   Going to be a good day?

JOSH   It's going to be great.

> *They commence running.*

Are we late?

BOWEY   Of course we are. We're always late.

JOSH   Right.

> *BOWEY and JOSH jump onto the wheel and run.*

COACH   Run you two! You run like *gerbils*! You think
              you'll be able to run like that when you get into
              the maze? You think it's going to be *soft*? You
              think it's going to be *easy*? You think you'll be
              able to *sleepwalk* through it like that? You take my
              word for it, you run like that you'll be gone for
              days. You run like that, the cheese will be eaten,
              the light filament will have gone out, and you'll
              still be in there *looking* around, *trying* to find your
              way, like the three blind mice. Aaargh! *Look* at
              you. I've seen *hamsters* that run faster than you,
              I've seen *newborn mice*, hairless, sightless, and
              toothless with more grit and gumption than that.
              You want to survive? Then *suck it up* and run!
              Run! Run!

> *The COACH exits.*

BOTH   I hate gym class.

JOSH   Bowey?

BOWEY   Yea?

JOSH	Do you ever wonder about this?
BOWEY	What?
JOSH	This.
BOWEY	No, I don't wonder about anything. You're not going to start asking a lot of questions are you? I don't know what good it does.
JOSH	It doesn't go anywhere you know.
BOWEY	What doesn't?
JOSH	The wheel.
BOWEY	No. But then, neither does the maze.
JOSH	Exactly.
BOWEY	Exactly what?
JOSH	Exactly *it doesn't go anywhere*.
BOWEY	Which is what makes the wheel such perfect training for the maze.

A bell sounds. They climb off the wheel.

Lunch.

JOSH	Thank heavens.
BOWEY	What have you got?
JOSH	What have I always got?
BOWEY	Sunflower seeds?
JOSH	Of course.
BOWEY	*Great!* Can I have one?
JOSH	That's what you always say.

BOWEY   Just one. Just *one*. Just a nibble.

JOSH   Take it.

BOWEY   Not hungry?

JOSH   No.

BOWEY   *Whoa. How* can you not be hungry? I'm always hungry. If I had my way I would carry a humongous sack of seeds with me wherever I went, and I mean *a great big honking sack*, at least as big as me, maybe bigger. I would *sit* on that sack of seeds during school, and I would eat all through class. I would carry it with me on the wheel and I would *run* with it, and I would eat the whole time I was running and when the gym teacher shouted at me I would spit the shells—poo!— right at him. Are you all right, you look tired?

JOSH   I *am* tired.

BOWEY   You worry too much. You got great big dark patches under your eyes, makes you look a bit like a, *chipmunk* or something.

JOSH   Thanks very much.

BOWEY   Seriously. You oughta' eat some cheese before you go to bed. Help you sleep.

JOSH   I spend most of my nights awake, which I suppose isn't so unusual. Mice are, after all, *nocturnal*, we're supposed to be awake nights.

BOWEY   Good point.

JOSH   Then again, what's the use of that? What exactly can you do in cage, at night, except let me see – oh yes, *nothing*.

Nothing but look around at the cage and the maze and the seeds and food pellets and the wheel, all laid out there in the dark, and all the other mice resting in the dark, waiting to get up and do their usual lab mouse business when the filament lights up, just like me. Nothing to do but stay awake, and listen to the sounds, and think.

BOWEY   You gotta try to relax.

JOSH   There's got to be something better than this, Bowey.

BOWEY   Than what?

JOSH   Than this.

BOWEY   This what?

JOSH   This. This. All this.

BOWEY   You mean, the cage?

JOSH   Yes.

BOWEY   What else is there?

JOSH   Well. What about, you know. Out there?

BOWEY   *(chuckles)* Out there? We know what's out there.

He meows.

JOSH   You think it's true?

BOWEY   You mean about,

He meows.

JOSH   Yes.

BOWEY   Absolutely.

BOTH   Yipes!

JOSH   But I mean, how many cars can there be out there?

BOWEY   *(laughs and punches JOSH)* Ha! You're such a kidder.

JOSH   Ow. What?

BOWEY   What do you mean what? You said "car."

JOSH   No I didn't.

BOWEY   Yea, you did. Car.

> *BOWEY punches JOSH.*

JOSH   Ow. I said cat. Why would I say "car?"

BOWEY   I don't know. But you did.

JOSH   Well I meant to say cat, and I've got to do something.

BOWEY   You sound serious.

JOSH   I *am* serious.

> *Beat.*

BOWEY   Well, y'know what you can do. And I'm not advising it, but, maybe you should see…

> *He drops his voice.*

The Sage.

JOSH   *(whispering)* The Sage?

BOTH   *(whispering)* Yes.

JOSH   Are you sure he exists?

BOWEY   Oh yea. Oh yea, he exists.

JOSH   Where?

BOWEY   Where else?

He drops his voice.

BOWEY   In the maze.

JOSH   The maze?

BOWEY   *That's* where he lives. They say my Great Grand Uncle Bernie saw him before he met up with the shock.

JOSH   How can anyone live in the maze? How can he survive?

BOWEY   That's what's *made* him so wise, living in the maze. He's unlocked all their mysterious secrets. He knows how to get past the traps, he knows where the food is. He's The Sage. The way I hear it, he knows the answer to *any* question.

JOSH   So he could answer my questions?

BOWEY   Yea, and maybe he's the only mouse who could. But the thing is… you have to go *looking* for him. In the maze. Which is like, impossible, cause you're too young.

The school bell rings.

Back to school.

BOWEY gets up and goes.

JOSH   Yea.

BOWEY   Josh?

JOSH seems lost in thought.

JOSH   Yea?

BOWEY   Coming? We got a ton of paper to shred.

JOSH   I'll be along in a bit.

BOWEY exits. JOSH stands up and scurries on over to the entrance of the mazes. He looks at the entrance to the yellow maze, the purple maze, and the red maze. He goes to the entrance of the yellow maze.

JOSH   Hello?

Hello, Mr. Sage? Can you hear me? Are you in there? Could you just come to the entrance here? I need to talk to you. I need to talk to *someone*.

Hello?

No answer. JOSH looks about, hesitates, then makes a decision and enters the yellow maze.

Hello? I'm just going to go a little way into the first maze. It can't be that hard, and if you could come talk to me that would... great. Okay. I'm just going a little way in.

JOSH hears something.

All right. I'm just a little way in. Can you hear me? Hello?

He goes in a bit further.

I'll go a little further.

When JOSH turns around, the SAGE has appeared.

Ah!

SAGE   What can I do for you?

JOSH   Ah. Well. That depends. Are you the Sage?

SAGE   And what would you do if I was?

JOSH   Ah well. I would. I would, ask you a question.

SAGE   You already have.

JOSH   Have what?

SAGE   Asked me a question. Almost the first thing you
           did. Ask another if you want.

JOSH   You haven't answered my first one.

SAGE   I only answer those questions which truly require
           an answer. Ask. And have a sunflower seed.

JOSH   Thanks. Um. I'm not sure how to begin.

SAGE   Just, start.

JOSH   The trouble is, I'm not sure I belong here.

SAGE   Uh huh.

JOSH   It's just. Everyone else seems happy. The cage
           doesn't bother them. I have, I don't know how
           many brothers, but *they* all seem satisfied.
           Nothing seems to bother *them*, but nothing
           makes sense to *me*.

SAGE   I see. I've counted a number of statements there,
           but have not detected any questions so far.

JOSH   Are you ever afraid?

SAGE   Yes.

JOSH   Because I am too. Of everything really. Of the
           light snapping on in the morning. The lights
           going out at night. The noise. The silence. The
           running around. The way that everyone seems
           to know what to do but I don't have a clue. Of
           what's in the cage, and what's outside the cage.
           Of the things I do know, and the things I don't.
           Everything. And I know mice aren't famous for
           being brave but, it can't be right to feel afraid all
           the time, can it? Not even for a mouse. And do
           you ever wonder what you're doing here?

SAGE	Okay. I'm going to ask *you* a question now. What *are* you doing here?
JOSH	What? Well, that's a, that's a – I mean, excuse me, but that's the question I asked *you*, how would I know the answer to that? I guess I'm doing what everyone else is doing.
SAGE	Are you?
JOSH	Well of course I am. Aren't I? Listen if you're just going to answer every question I've got with another question, that's not going to help much. Hello?

The SAGE is gone.

Hello? Hello? *Hello?* Where did you go? Hello?

One of JOSH's brothers appears.

BROTHER	Hi.
JOSH	*(startled)* Ah!
BROTHER	Josh, what are you doing in the maze?
JOSH	I was just talking to, someone.
BROTHER	Talking to someone? Here? Who?
JOSH	He's gone.
BROTHER	I didn't see anyone coming back my way.
JOSH	He was right *here*.
BROTHER	You're too young to be in the maze. You better get back home.
JOSH	Yea.

They walk back together.

JOSH   You're Jesse, aren't you?

BROTHER Jonathon.

JOSH   Right. Yes, of course. I knew that. And which brother are–

BROTHER The nineteenth.

JOSH   Right. Yes. Nineteenth. Don't mention I was here to Mom or Dad, okay?

Lights out. Lights snap back up.

MAMA   Josh. Can you please make your bed?

JOSH   Yes.

JOSH takes a few pawfuls of wood shavings and liberally tosses them about.

There.

MAMA   Thank you. Are you all right?

JOSH   What do you mean?

MAMA   You seem, distant. Like you're thinking about something else all the time.

JOSH   I'm fine. I just don't understand so many things. I feel–

MAMA   I wouldn't worry so much. We mice aren't supposed to be too introspective. We try to stay active. Get a little lettuce in your diet, are you getting any lettuce in your diet?

JOSH   Yes.

MAMA   And make sure you get enough sleep. Are you getting enough sleep?

JOSH   Yea. Sure.

MAMA	I'm not certain that you are. Have you cleaned up for bed?
JOSH	Yea.
MAMA	And behind your ears?

She inspects.

You missed a spot.

She quickly licks behind his ears.

JOSH	Mom!
MAMA	*(singing)* When darkness falls And all your thoughts Crowd around your head. Remember that is what The purpose is of your bed...

Go to sleep
Close your eyes
Stay at peace
Till you rise
With the light

Close your eyes
Ease your mind
Leave your thoughts
and your worries behind.

Close your eyes.
Ease your mind.
Go to sleep.

MAMA turns to go.

JOSH	Mom?
MAMA	Yes.
JOSH	Are *you* ever afraid?

MAMA   Sh. Go to sleep. I've got to tuck in your other brothers.

JOSH   But *are* you? Do you ever think about things and just get, scared?

MAMA   Sometimes.

JOSH   And when you do?

MAMA   *(slight beat)* I get busy with something.

JOSH   Like what?

MAMA   There's always something to get busy with.

    She stands.

JOSH   Mom? How come we don't use the number three?

    Pause.

MAMA   What do you mean?

JOSH   How come I don't have a third brother? I'm the fourth, but there's no three.

MAMA   It's late.

JOSH   But, how does that make sense?

MAMA   We can talk about that another time.

JOSH   But–

MAMA   Sh.

JOSH   Why don't we use–

MAMA   Get some sleep. And make sure you eat your lettuce. I just want you to be happy, Josh.

    Now rest. Good night.

She exits.

JOSH   Good night.

                Lights up.

FATHER   Ah!

                *Shrieking with terror, the FATHER sits up, and
                then, realizing what time it is, he shrieks again.*

                Ah!

                *He leaps from his bed of wood chips and ripped
                cardboard. Startled by the cries of her husband,
                MAMA awakens as well and leaps out of the
                wood chips.*

MAMA   Ah!

                *JOSH sits straight up from his bed of wood chips,
                startled and alarmed as well.*

JOSH   Ah!

FATHER   I'm gonna' be late!

                *Both MAMA and FATHER race about in frantic
                circles. JOSH continues to sit, blinking.*

MAMA   Get up. Get up. The lab lights have come on.

                *She races around the cage in the opposite direction
                from FATHER, throwing around every bit as
                much sawdust and debris as he does.*

MAMA   You'll–

FATHER   I'll–

BOTH   –be late.

MAMA   Come on, get up. I've made some breakfast. Have
                a pumpkin seed.

She throws him a pumpkin seed.

FATHER   No time.

> *He throws it back.*

MAMA   At *least* have a drink from the water applicator.

> *FATHER races to the water applicator and drinks and gargles loudly. JOSH rises from his wood chips looking very sleepy.*

JOSH   I'm up.

MAMA   Have you washed?

> *She begins to vigorously lick behind his ears.*

JOSH   Ma!

> *FATHER goes to the wheel and runs on it. BROTHER jumps up out of the shavings.*

BROTHER   Oh-my-gosh, look at the time.

JOSH   Dad!

FATHER   What?

JOSH   Isn't there something you're doing that you shouldn't be?

FATHER   What?

JOSH   You're *running in the same spot*, it's always the same thing, can't you see you're *always* running in the same spot? Can't you see that?

> *Beat.*

FATHER   Right. Thanks.

> *He gets off the wheel.*

FATHER	How do I look?
MAMA	Great.

       MAMA and FATHER quickly rub noses.

FATHER	Bye.
MAMA	Are you all right?
JOSH	I'm fine.
BROTHER	Can I have some lunch to take with me?
FATHER	Come on. We're going to be late for the maze.
MAMA	Here's a raisin.

       BROTHER takes the raisin and races off through the tunnels. JOSH and MAMA are left in the relative calm aftermath of the departure.

JOSH	Which one is he again?
MAMA	Number 12. Lewis.
JOSH	Right. I better go.

      JOSH starts off for school and is met by BOWEY.

BOWEY	Hey! Wait up.

      BOWEY catches up with JOSH and they perform their special handshaking ritual, although JOSH seems a bit dispirited in his execution of it. It ends, as usual, with:

JOSH & BOWEY	Smooooth.
BOWEY	Going to be a good day?
JOSH	I hope.

BOWEY	Hey! Is it going to be a good day?
JOSH	Yes. It's going to be great. Couldn't be better.
BOWEY	Okay. Hey, where did you go yesterday?
JOSH	I skipped class.
BOWEY	You're kidding? Are you kidding me? You are *so* behind in ripping up paper. I don't know how you'll catch up. Do you know what'll happen if you keep falling behind?
JOSH	Nothing.
BOWEY	Nothing?
JOSH	Because none of it really matters.
BOWEY	Ya, I suppose that's true, but I always thought that was the upside to it. So, where did you go?
JOSH	I went looking for the Sage.
BOWEY	You're *kidding*? In the mazes?
JOSH	Yes.
BOWEY	Did you. Did you see, *him*?
JOSH	Yes.
BOWEY	Whoa. What did he tell you?
JOSH	I didn't get a chance to talk to him long. He disappeared.
BOWEY	Disappeared?
JOSH	Yea.
BOWEY	Whoa. Hey where are you going?
JOSH	I'm going to see him again if I can.

BOWEY   Are you *kidding*? Are you nuts? Are you crazy?

JOSH   I've got to get him to *answer* my questions this time.

BOWEY   But don't you know?

JOSH   Know what?

BOWEY   The way I've heard it, passed on from my Great Grand Uncle Bernie, with each question you ask, depending upon how difficult it is, you have to travel into a more difficult part of the maze. You can get totally lost asking the really difficult questions.

JOSH keeps going, BOWEY runs to keep up.

I mean, yesterday it was probably a yellow maze, right? Today, it'll be the *purple*.

JOSH   So?

BOWEY   So, you'll get *lost*. No one will *find you* – until you're nothing but mouse skin and mouse bones. Mouse claws. A couple of mouse teeth. A little mouse dandruff.

He shudders.

JOSH   Not if you help me.

BOWEY   *What*?

JOSH   Look. We both take handfuls of seeds, and we drop them as we go. That way we can find our way back out by following the trail of seeds.

BOWEY   What happens when we run out of seeds?

JOSH   Then, we'll turn back.

BOWEY hesitates.

BOWEY	I don't know if it's that simple.
JOSH	I've got to talk to him. It's important.
BOTH	Why?
JOSH	It just *is*. I can't be running in the same spot anymore.
BOWEY	What's wrong with running in the same spot, you don't need a map, you don't have to put on a coat—
JOSH	—Are you with me or not?
BOWEY	All right. I'll do it. Because you're a friend. And you share your lunch with me. But just this *once*. And *only for a little while*.

They arrive at the maze.

Ew, I don't like this.

They enter the purple maze.

It's quiet. Too quiet.

JOSH	Yesterday, all I had to do was call. Hello? Hello?
BOWEY	Hello?
JOSH	Hello?
BOWEY	No one here. Oh well—

BOWEY begins to walk away. JOSH stops him.

JOSH	Maybe we should go a little further in. So, which way?
BOWEY	It's a *maze*, Josh. There are no signs. Pick a direction.
JOSH	This way.

BOWEY   I hope you know what you're doing.

JOSH   Then, we'll turn here. And here. And I'll bet if we turn here it will lead us to a—

                They arrive at a dead end.

BOWEY   —dead end.

JOSH   Okay. That's *good*. Process of elimination, right? That's one way we *won't* go. We'll go *this* way instead. And look, it goes straight on this time. This feels better. I'm feeling much more confident.

BOWEY   Yea.

JOSH   We turn right.

BOWEY   Good.

JOSH   And then left.

BOWEY   Also good.

JOSH   And then right—

                They come upon the skeleton of a mouse.

BOWEY   Into the scary mouse skeleton.

BOTH   The scary mouse skeleton!

                Both scream and run. Finally they stop and rest, panting.

JOSH   That was, ah, completely frightening.

BOWEY   Yea. Josh, don't ever. *Ever.* Lead me to a place that a *skeleton* has gotten to first.

JOSH   I am *so* glad we left that behind.

BOWEY   No kidding.

JOSH   Ya, we left it *way* behind.

BOWEY   *Way* behind.

JOSH   We left it so far behind.

BOWEY   So far behind–

JOSH   That now we're good and–

BOWEY   *(freaking out)* –Lost. *All* our seeds were dropped
            back there!

JOSH   *(another moment of panic)* All our seeds!

                Followed by quick recovery.

            Don't worry. That's okay. Once we find the Sage,
            he'll be able to help us.

BOWEY   Yea. That's right. That's good. Now all we have
            to do is find him. Hello? Hello, Mr. Sage?
            Helloooo?

JOSH   Hello?

BOWEY   Hello?

JOSH   Hello?

BOWEY   Why isn't he answering?

JOSH   I'm sure there's a good reason, and look there's a
            fork in the maze.

BOWEY   We can save time, if we split up and each take a
            peek down the tunnel. If we don't see anyone,
            then we come right back. Right?

JOSH   Right.

                They split up.

BOWEY   Josh!

JOSH	Yes?
BOWEY	Don't go far.
JOSH	I won't.

They start to go.

BOWEY	And Josh.
JOSH	What?
BOWEY	I want a hug.
JOSH	All right!

They hug.

Now get going.

JOSH turns around, and who should be there but... the SAGE.

SAGE	Can I be of any help?
JOSH	Ah! It's you!
SAGE	You were looking for me?
JOSH	That's right. Bowey, you can come back now! Bowey!
SAGE	What did you want?
JOSH	The thing is, I think I have to do something and I need you to help me figure out what it is I have to do.
SAGE	You have your friend down the tunnel. You have your family.
JOSH	Yes. But... but.... But can I tell you a secret?
SAGE	If you like.

JOSH   I told you I was afraid. I think my family is too, and they don't even know it. So how can *they* help me?

I told you I have more brothers than I can keep track of.

SAGE   Yes?

JOSH   I don't think my parents can either. There's no third brother. I'm the fourth. There's no number three. How can that be?

SAGE   So what do you want?

JOSH   Tell me what to do.

SAGE   I can't.

                Beat.

JOSH   Maybe I have to leave the cage.

SAGE   Why do you say that?

JOSH   It just came to me.

SAGE   Well, maybe you do.

JOSH   But what about the dangers out there?

SAGE   I suppose if it seems too risky, you'll have to stay.

JOSH   I can't do that either.

SAGE   Then go.

JOSH   But I don't even know how to get out.

SAGE   When you're ready to leave. You'll know.

BOWEY   *(calling from off)* Josh.

JOSH   I'm over here.

The SAGE disappears.

When I'm ready to leave, I'll know. What kind of answer is that? Hello? Hey, where did he go?

Hello?

Enter BOWEY.

BOWEY   Did you find him?

JOSH   Yes.

BOWEY   Well where is he?

JOSH   I lost him again.

BOWEY   How could you *lose* him? That's so totally *careless.* You couldn't have found him for more than a couple of minutes.

JOSH   I don't know!

BOWEY   What did you do? Did you throw him down a hole or something?

JOSH   I'm telling you I don't know! He was here and then he was *gone.* Maybe that's the way it is with Sages, they kinda' disappear at will.

BOWEY   Well that's just great. No seeds, no sage, here we are stuck in the maze, and it's only a couple of hours till dinner. Did you at least ask him your questions?

JOSH   Yes.

BOWEY   So do you feel better?

JOSH   No.

BOWEY   Why? What did he say?

JOSH   He said I can get out anytime.

BOWEY	That's good. How?
JOSH	He neglected to reveal that part.
BOWEY	Well that's just perfect. Now what?
JOSH	He said when I was ready to leave I'd be able to get out.
BOWEY	Well tell me when you're ready, cause I'm ready right now. I am *so* ready.
JOSH	How can he say that?
BOWEY	I am completely, one hundred percent, beginning to end, start to finish, *ready* to leave this maze.
JOSH	Unless.
BOWEY	Unless what?
JOSH	Unless it's easier to get out than we think.
BOWEY	S'cuse me. It's the *maze* we're talking about. The *maze*. The whole point of a maze is *they're not easy to get out of*!
JOSH	But he did, didn't he? Just now. Got out of it. He just, disappeared, right?
BOWEY	Right. But, like you were saying – he's the Sage.
JOSH	But. Maybe, like, he's saying, that *anyone* can leave, when they want.
BOWEY	Is that what he said?
JOSH	Well, it's not *exactly* what he said, but–
BOWEY	But *what*?
JOSH	Maybe we should try feeling for openings.
BOWEY	What do you mean, *feel* for openings?

JOSH   You know, *doors*. Secret compartments. Escape
                hatches. Maybe they're built in, you know, to the
                walls.

BOWEY   I hardly think so.

JOSH   Let's just try.

BOWEY   Fine.

                They push at the walls.

BOWEY   I'll try, although. I don't even know *what* I'm
                looking for.

JOSH   For a panel. Or a hatch. Or button. A way out.
                Are you pushing?

BOWEY   I'm *pushing*. I don't know why I'm pushing, but
                I'm pushing. I don't know why I let you talk me
                into going into this maze in the first place. I *said*
                it's the maze. It's gonna' be difficult. But no, no,
                no. You had to go in. You *had* to go in.

JOSH   Just keep pushing.

BOWEY   I *said* I'm pushing.

JOSH   There.

                *JOSH pushes on a panel and out he goes. There's
                a sound in the background – perhaps like wind
                blowing.*

                I made it. That wasn't so hard. He was right.
                There's a way out, see?

                He glances about.

                This is different.

                He looks around but BOWEY is nowhere about.

Bowey? You can come through now. Bowey?
Bowey?

> *No answer. JOSH tries to push back in, but can't.*
> *The SAGE appears.*

Can you hear me? Bowey?

> *He pounds on the wall.*

Bowey?

SAGE   You made it.

> *JOSH turns.*

JOSH   Yea. I made it. But I can't get back in now.

SAGE   There's no going back.

JOSH   What do you mean there's no going back? I never
would have come here if I knew there was no
going back. Bowey?

SAGE   Some journeys are one way journeys.

JOSH   Oh yea? What kind of journeys are those?

SAGE   The journey of knowledge is like that.

JOSH   "The Journey of Knowledge?" What kind of
stupid journey is that? "Journey of Knowledge,"
"Journey of Knowledge" – no one told *me* you
can't go back.

SAGE   No. No one said that–

JOSH   Hey, inside? Let me in. Let me in.

SAGE   –but that's the way it is.

> *He hears a sound. The sound of wind. Or*
> *breathing. The sound of air moving. The sound he*
> *heard earlier when everyone else was asleep.*

> *Throughout this passage, the SAGE begins to take on more human qualities and lose his mouse qualities.*

JOSH   Listen, that sound. Did you hear that? What is that?

SAGE   What do you think it is?

JOSH   I don't know. But I don't like it. That's one scary sound.

                Is it a cat?

                He listens. It grows louder.

                I think it's a cat.

                He makes as if to run.

SAGE   Wait. Just listen.

                They listen.

JOSH   What is it?

SAGE   You know.

JOSH   Will you *stop* that. If I *knew*, would I *ask* you?

SAGE   Sh.

                They listen.

JOSH   It could be a cat.

SAGE   Listen.

                He listens.

JOSH   Doesn't sound like a cat.

SAGE   What does it sound like?

JOSH	It sounds like a. Like a. Like a, car.

      Beat.

      It sounds like a car.

      Beat.

      That scares me even more. Why is that?

SAGE	I don't have to tell you.
JOSH	But I *want* you to tell me. I *want* you to tell me – that's why I'm asking you. I mean, it seems dangerous. *Everything* seems dangerous out here, wherever this is.
SAGE	Not everything.
JOSH	Yes! *Everything* – I mean, how else can you explain how a day can start off perfect. Everything perfect and then go so wrong. How can you start off as the fourth of four brothers, and then end up…

      Beat.

      I want to go back in now.

SAGE	You can't. What were you going to say?
JOSH	Nothing. I just want to go back in. Let me in.

      He tries to return.

      Hello? Bowey? Can you hear me? Let me in.

SAGE	What were you going to say?
JOSH	*Nothing.*
SAGE	You were going to say something.
JOSH	I wasn't going to say anything–

SAGE   You were. Say it. Say it.

JOSH   I was just going to say how can you start off as
                the fourth of four brothers, and then end up with
                only three. That's just, mathematically impossible
                isn't it?

                How can that be possible?

                   He thinks a moment, and stops.

                I remember.

SAGE   What?

JOSH   My third brother.

                It was a perfectly normal, day. I'd already gone to
                school. He was supposed to follow. He was late.
                He was always late. But this time he never
                showed up. All day long I wondered where he
                was. What had happened. And then they told me
                at school. And they sent me home. And every-
                thing had *changed*. He was, just gone. Like this,
                hole, he fell into. He was gone, and everybody
                kept right on *doing things* like nothing had hap-
                pened, like he never stepped out on the street,
                never got hit by a car. How could he be gone?
                How could I go to school with him following me
                one moment – and then go home, and never see
                him again? How could that make sense?

SAGE   Sometimes things happen that don't make sense.

JOSH   Well what kind of crazy, useless system is that?

SAGE   It's hard to believe it when you lose someone.

JOSH   *Lose* someone? How do you *lose* someone? You
                don't just *lose* a brother. It's not like a seed that
                you just drop and forget about. "Oh, seems I lost
                a brother, not in my pockets. Wonder where I put
                him."

	Oh. It's dangerous out here. It's so dangerous.
SAGE	Absolutely.
JOSH	And nobody ever wants to talk about it. You know? Everyone has *stuff* to do. "Stuff." Everyone's running around, like, like, like mice. In a cage. Running around and around and around. Everybody's busy. All the time. Everybody always has something to do.
	How? How could they have anything to do?
	Didn't they know my brother was gone, and that changed everything?
SAGE	Well. Everybody *is* busy. There always *is* something to do. And on another level everybody's scared. Nobody wants to stop and think about it when something bad happens.
JOSH	How do *you* stop? How do you stop being scared?
SAGE	A little at a time. A bit more each day. What is it that scares you?
JOSH	It's big out here. It feels empty without him.
	It sinks in.
	Oh man, it feels *so* empty.
	And I can't change anything.
SAGE	Who said that? Who said you can't change anything? You can't change *everything*. Some things you can't change on your own.
JOSH	Am I ever going to get out?
SAGE	You *are* out.
JOSH	What?

SAGE	You're out of the cage. Now you have to live here.
JOSH	You think I can?
SAGE	I know you can. Look.

As the SAGE says "look," the cage begins to transform. The walls of the cage fold down, and the cage turns into a home. When JOSH's family appear, they have lost their mouse ears, tails and noses — they are humans. JOSH removes his mouse nose, ears and tail.

You were never in.

MAMA appears without mouse ears or tail. JOSH and she share a conversation as the SAGE looks on. MAMA can't see the SAGE.

MAMA	Morning.
JOSH	Morning.
MAMA	Have you got your lunch?
JOSH	*(to the SAGE)* But what do I do, out here, when I'm lost?
SAGE	Breathe. And trust yourself.
MAMA	Josh?
SAGE	You'll find your way.
JOSH	Yea, I've got it. Can I take a cookie?
MAMA	Go ahead. Leave two for your brothers.
	And can you do something with your hair?
JOSH	It's fine.

She licks her thumb and smoothes down a portion.

MAMA	Josh. Try not to worry so much.
JOSH	I'm trying. I really am.
MAMA	I know you are. I know you are. Now hurry. Bowey's waiting for you.

> *JOSH leaves.*

JOSH	*(to the SAGE)* It still feels, empty. Does it ever stop feeling that way?
SAGE	Bit by bit. Have patience. Now go on. You'll be okay.

> *The SAGE exits, and JOSH proceeds to where BOWEY is waiting. He too has no mouse ears or tail or nose. In every other way he is still BOWEY.*

BOWEY	Hey – you finished your homework?
JOSH	Ya. Here.
BOWEY	Whoa, what did you do? Gnaw on it?
JOSH	It got slightly mangled getting from one place to another.
BOWEY	What have you got in your lunch pack? Do you have a cheese sandwich?
JOSH	Yes.
BOWEY	Oh *yes*! That's what I like to hear!

> *He initiates their greeting ritual culminating in:*

BOTH	Smoooth!
BOWEY	Is it going to be a good day?
JOSH	Going to be a great day.

BOWEY   Excellent. Let's go we're late.

JOSH   Right.

BOWEY   How about a nibble of that sandwich?

JOSH   That's what you always say.

BOWEY   Just one. Just *one*. Just a nibble. It's not like I'm going to eat it all.

> *They walk together, across the street and on their way.*

> *The end.*

photo by Agamdeep Darshi

Clem Martini writes for both stage and screen, but is best known for his darkly comic vision of life presented in plays such as *The Life History of the African Elephant, Illegal Entry, Conversations With My Neighbour's Pitbull, Up On The Roof* and *Selling Mr. Rushdie*. He is a three-time winner of the Writer's Guild of Alberta Award, a National Theatre Competition Award Winner, and a Governor General Nominee. When not at his desk writing, Mr. Martini can be found teaching at the University of Calgary, or working with troubled young people through the charitable organization, Woods Homes. Other published works by Clem Martini include: *Something Like A Drug – The Oral History of Theatresports* (co-authored), *Turn Around* (co-authored), *Illegal Entry*, and *A Three Martini Lunch*.